РУССКІЙ МУЗЕЙ
ИМПЕРАТОРА АЛЕКСАНДРА ТРЕТЬЯГО
ОСНОВАНЪ 13 АПРѢЛЯ 1895г. — ОТКРЫТЪ 7 МАРТА 1898г.

THE STATE RUSSIAN MUSEUM

THE RUSSIAN MUSEUM

A CENTENNIAL CELEBRATION
OF A NATIONAL TREASURE

PALACE EDITIONS

Editor-in-Chief
Yevgenia Petrova

Authors of Text
Vladimir Gusyev (V. G.)
Yevgenia Petrova (Y. P.)

Artistic Director
Joseph Kiblitsky

Editor of the Russian Text
Anna Laks

Translation from the Russian
Kenneth MacInnes

General Preparation
Alla Rodina

Proofreader
Irina Tokareva

Computer Graphics
Yekaterina Sivtsova

Assistants
Rufina Aminova
Cosmo Masiello
Maurizio Supino

Photographers
Vladimir Dorokhov
Valery Kyuner
Vasily Vorontsov

Published by
Joseph Kiblitsky

Distributed by
Harry N. Abrams Inc.,
Publishers

ЛР № 040692
ISBN 0-8109-6357-4 (Abrams)
ISBN 5-900872-44-0 (Russia)
ISBN 3-930775-36-0 (Germany)

Published in 1998
by the State Russian Museum,
St. Peterburg

Distributed in 1998
by Harry N. Abrams,
Incorporated, New York

Printed and bound in Italy
by GRAFICART - Formia (LT)

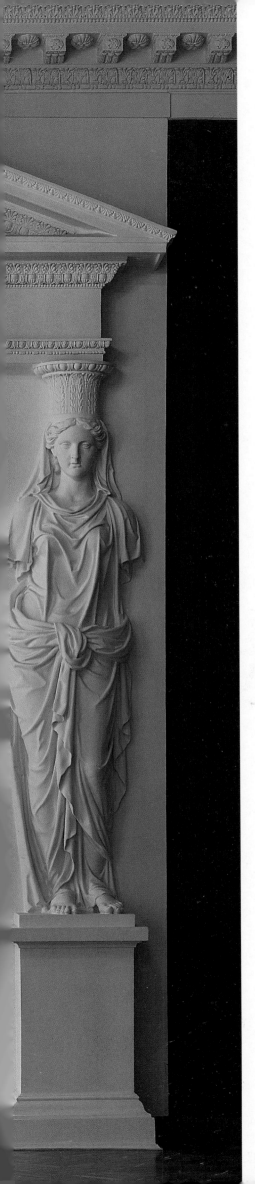

CONTENTS

THE HISTORY OF THE MUSEUM

On April 13th 1895, not long after the death of Emperor Alexander III, his son and heir Nicholas II signed a Decree On The Establishment Of A Museum of Russian Fine Art In The Capital Of The Russian Empire In Memory Of Our Father.

Three years later, on March 7th 1898, the doors of the Mikhailovsky Palace in St Petersburg

ly be highly desirable here in Russia ... Construction of a new museum is vital to the history of our national art" were the words of a report made by Alexander Vasilchikov, director of the Hermitage, in 1881.

The calls for a national art gallery were supposedly "stirred" by the coinciding of the patriotic aspirations of both liberal society and Emperor

Karl Beggroff. The Mikhailovsky Palace. 1832

opened to welcome visitors to Russia's first ever state museum of national fine art.

The necessity of a national art museum for Russia had already become acute towards the end of the nineteenth century. Neither the museums of St Petersburg (the Russian Picture Gallery in the Hermitage, the Museum of the Academy of Arts) nor Moscow (the Public Rumyantsev Museum, the Tretyakov Gallery) possessed collections offering a complete picture of the history of Russian art. "The organization of an exclusively Russian public picture gallery would undoubted-

Alexander III, who – as was officially cultivated – was said to be a connoisseur and patron of Russian art.

A fitting building was soon found for the new museum – the Mikhailovsky Palace, built for the Emperor Paul's youngest son Mikhail and a unique monument to early nineteenth-century Classical Russian architecture.

A striking view opens up from St Petersburg's central magistral – Nevsky Prospekt – onto the main palace facade, with its well-proportioned and elegant eight-columned Corinthian portico.

The palace was designed and built by Karl Rossi (1777–1849). Rossi was the genius behind the architectural ensembles in the Empire style that added the finishing touches to the centre of St Petersburg in the 1810s and 1820s.

The initial collection of painting, sculpture, drawings and applied art numbered around 1,500 works. The accompanying collection of Christian art from Novgorod. The Emperor acquired the collection of Prince Alexei Lobanov-Rostovsky (1824–1896) from the Prince's heirs and presented it to the Russian Museum. The portraits of Russian eighteenth and early nineteenth century statesmen present the most interest here. A large part of the museum's extensive collection of water-colours and drawings by Russian artists

Luigi Premazzi. *Grand Duke Mikhail Pavlovich's Study in the Mikhailovsky Palace. 1856*

antiquities contained some five thousand exhibits. The Hermitage presented the museum with practically its entire gallery of Russian paintings, its collection of sculpture and part of its collection of drawings and water-colours. Paintings, sculptures, water-colours, drawings, engravings and cartoons were also donated by the Museum of the Academy of Arts.

The Academy of Arts also offered its entire Museum of Christian Antiquities, established in 1858. Whilst this collection was not terribly large, it nevertheless contained some very valuable pieces, amongst them icons, wooden sculptures and ancient and medieval works of applied was presented by Princess Maria Tenisheva. This section was put together and systematized with the help of the artist and art critic Alexander Benois. Finally, there was the major contribution of the personal collection of Alexander III, from the Alexander Palace in Tsarskoye Selo (items from the Anichkov Palace entered the museum much later).

The Russian Museum's first decade thus saw its collection almost double in size. Considerable additions were made to the collections of engravings and drawings. The acquisition of the celebrated collection of Russian and Greek icons belonging to the historian and collector Nikolai

Likhachev (1862–1936) greatly enlarged the department of Christian antiquities. This permitted its transformation into the Archive of Monuments of Russian Icon-painting and Ecclesiastical Antiquities in 1914, at the time Russia's largest state collection of icons. Many fine works were also presented to the museum by the owners of private collections.

the Russian Museum and the Tretyakov Gallery thus all swapped exhibits.

Of course, it would have been better if Russia had escaped the turmoil of revolution and works had found their way into the Russian Museum by a more natural and settled, if longer, route. History, however, does not recognise subjunctive moods, and today one can only assert that the

St Michael's Castle. Northern façade

In 1917 revolution shook Russia. In all fairness to history, however, it must be said that the Russian Museum came out of the upheavals relatively unscathed. Indeed, the decade following the revolution witnessed a rapid growth in the museum's collection. As before, there were major acquisitions from the Imperial palaces – the Winter Palace, the Anichkov Palace, the Gatchina Palace and the Marble Palace. The Russian Museum's collection was considerably added to by items received in 1923 from the Academy of Arts. A redistribution of archives about different museums was effected, in accordance with the specific nature of each museum. The Hermitage,

museum archives represented salvation for many thousands of works of art remaining behind in the appropriated or looted palaces, estates and apartments. Many collectors were forced to either donate or sell their collections and the museum walls were the sole guarantee that their collections and the names of those who had put them together would be preserved for posterity. Today the museum is home to the world's largest collection of Russian fine art. It is unique in both the extent of its chronological boundaries, stretching from the start of the eleventh century right up to the present day, and in the fact that it covers practically every area of the fine arts. Unsurprisingly, the Mikhailovsky Palace soon proved too small for the simultaneous storage and display of such an enormous, growing collection. In recent years, however, the situation has eased somewhat. The Mayor's Office has presented the museum with three new palaces in the centre of St Petersburg.

The eldest of the three – the Stroganov Palace –

sent for Count Grigory Orlov. Later, in the nineteenth century, it was the residence of various Grand Dukes. The last of them, Grand Duke Konstantin Konstantinovich, was a famous Silver Age poet, who wrote under the pseudonym of K. R. (Konstantin Romanov). After the revolution, in another paradox of Russian history, this fine monument of early Classicism was turned into a

View onto the Stroganov Palace from the Police Bridge. Engraving. 1840s–1850s

stands on the corner of Nevsky Prospekt and the Moika embankment. It was built for Baron Sergei Stroganov in 1753 by Francesco Bartolomeo Rastrelli, son of an Italian sculptor invited to Russia by Peter the Great.

The Stroganov Palace is a fine example of Russian Baroque; original, colourful and distinct from West European Baroque. It was owned by many generations of Stroganovs, one of Russia's oldest and most illustrious families. The pride of the building is possibly the Large Ballroom, one of Rastrelli's few surviving interiors, with its enormous plafond by Giuseppe Valeriani, the second largest in Europe.

The Marble Palace was built between 1768 and 1785 by the Italian architect Antonio Rinaldi. Catherine the Great intended the palace as a pre-

Lenin Museum, dedicated to the revolutionary who had coined the slogan "Peace to the peasant huts, war on the palaces". Yet every cloud has a silver lining, and the transformation of the Marble Palace into a museum meant that the building itself was preserved remarkably well.

The architecture of the romantic and enigmatic Engineers' Castle reflects the tragic personality of its royal owner – the Emperor Paul. It was his architectural fantasies that lay at the heart of the project, realized between 1797 and 1801 by the Italian Vincenzo Brenna with help from Vasily Bazhenov. The palace façades have survived to the present day almost unchanged. Many interiors have also been preserved – the Main Staircase, the Maltese and Throne Rooms overlooking Connetable Square, and the Church of the

Archangel Michael. Legend has it that the Archangel Michael, divine protector of the House of Romanov, appeared to Paul in a dream. The angel allegedly told Paul where he ought to build his new palace, whence its original name – St Michael's Castle. It earned its other name

threshold of its second century, with plans for the creation of a wide complex of expositions in each palace. The aim of this new complex of old palaces is to reflect both the wealth of the collection of the Russian Museum and to offer a complete picture of the history of Russian art.

Marble Palace (from the Neva Embankment). Northern facade

when Russia's oldest School of Military Engineering moved into it following Paul's murder. These three palaces now constitute a new and historical ensemble, united by the Russian Museum. And now the museum stands on the

Not every museum has the possibility of using its exposition to display the many centuries of its national art history. The Russian Museum enjoys such a possibility, and we hope that this album will be confirmation of this. (*V. G.*)

Icons, Old Russian Applied Art

Many who have not been to St Petersburg mistakenly think that the Russian Museum is part of the Hermitage. In actual fact, the Russian Museum is a completely independent, vast collection of almost 400,000 works. It is the world's largest collection of Russian art, roughly five times the size of that of the Tretyakov Gallery in Moscow. The collection of the Russian Museum includes painting, sculpture, graphic art, decorative-applied art, folk art and numismatics. It embraces all forms of art that have developed over Russia's history, from the adoption of Christianity in 989 to the current day.

The Russian Museum possesses more than five thousand icons, as well as some one and a half thousand works of medieval jewellery, ecclesiastical utensils and religious objects. Ecclesiastical art represents almost seven centuries of Russian culture. Until the start of the eighteenth centu-

ry, art in Russia was mainly based on religious presentments of the world. Early Russian history was a series of stormy events – wars, power struggles, and the rise and fall of various states. This was accompanied by the construction and reconstruction of churches, monasteries and cathedrals. For Russians, mundane life was only the beginning, a preparation for a better, posthumous life. Important events – victories or defeats in battle, the birth or death of a member of the leading dynasties – were usually marked by the construction of a church, or gifts ("endowments") to the church. The events of everyday life in this way told on the architecture and internal appointments of churches, monasteries and cathedrals. Therefore the icons of the Novgorod, Pskov, Archangel and Muscovite masters, which might at first glance seem relatively similar, in reality tell the story of six centuries of Russian history.

Bracelets (ryasni)
First Half of the 12th Century

Pendants (kolti) with Birds
Late 12th – Early 13th Centuries

The oldest icon in the collection of the Russian Museum is *The Archangel Gabriel (The Angel with Golden Hair)*. It was painted in the twelfth century. The head of the angel, with its large almond-shaped eyes, commands the entire icon. Monumental for all its small dimensions, emphasis is laid on the contour of the angel's face. More decorative and splendid is the golden hair framing the archangel's head and shoulders. Who painted the icon and how and when it came to be in a Russian church remains a mystery. But the presence of golden threads – symbol of the majesty and immortality of the Olympian gods – betray Hellenistic traditions, the heir to which in the Middle Ages was Byzantium. One notable feature of the collection of the Russian Museum is its relatively large number of icons from the north of Russia. Novgorod, Pskov, Vologda, Belozersk and Arkhangelsk all lie relatively close to St Petersburg and so are well represented in its collection of icons. *The Mother of God of Belozersk* is an early thirteenth century icon and an extremely rare and ancient work of art. Its iconography – The Mother of God of Tenderness (the Christ child embraces His mother, brushing her cheek with His face) – had been established in Byzantium before the twelfth century. The representations in the margins of the icon date back to an even older tradition.

Bracelet. Late 12th – Early 13th Centuries

The *Boris and Gleb* icon (mid-14th century, Muscovy) is one of the most striking of medieval monuments in the museum collection. Boris's deep blue cloak and its golden ornamental design shine forth, lending the icon a solemn and festive air.

Boris and Gleb were two brothers, the sons of Prince Vladimir, founder of Christianity in Rus. Intestine strife broke out following his death and both brothers were killed. Boris and Gleb were subsequently revered in Russia as defenders of the faith. From the eleventh century onwards, historical compositions were devoted to them, churches built in their honour and conjectural portraits painted. The icon portrays the two brothers together with their habitual attributes – a cross (symbol of martyrdom) and a sword (personifying power and protection). All schools of icon-painting in medieval Rus, a time when each major town followed its own traditions, are re-

Pendants (kolti) with Birds
First Half of the 12th Century

Master Grigory
Patriarch Pitirim's Glass.
Novgorod 1672.

presented in the Russian Museum. Amongst the magnificent red and gold icons of Novgorod *The Battle between Novgorod and Suzdal* is of particular note. It is unique not only for its colour and compositional scheme, but also its subject. The icon is based on a true historical event and represents one of Russia's first history paintings.

The Resurrection – The Descent into Hell is an icon from Pskov (late 14th century). Christ has risen and is leading King David, King Solomon and other Old Testament patriarchs out of the black abyss of Hell. This subject was fairly popular in Russian icons, though in the Pskov icon it takes on a particularly dramatic note. The contrasts between the black, red and gold tones and the sharp, awkward movements of the crouching figures add tension and gravity to the scene. The only festive notes are the bright white brush strokes on the faces and clothes, giving the impression of dimension. The golden assists covering the details of the vestments add a touch of opulence to the icon's simple and laconic colour scheme.

The piety of the northern icons is repeated in the terse and monumental works of the Muscovite masters. The rather menacing title of one of them – *The Saviour Furious Eye* (late 14th – early 15th centuries) – reflects an iconographic type popular amongst the Old Believers. It emphasized the role of Christ as the judge of mankind. Such icons were popular in Russia during the Time of Troubles, when the Orthodox church split into those faithful to the old canons and those who advocated its reformation. The soft, smooth silhouette of Christ's face, the elegant colour combinations and three-dimensional form are typical of other Muscovy icons painted in the fourteenth and fifteenth centuries. The collection of the Russian Museum is particularly rich in icons by such leading Muscovite masters as Andrei Rublev. *St Paul the Apostle* (circa 1408) and its pair *St Peter the Apostle* come from the deēsus line of the Church of the Dormition of the Mother of God in Vladimir. When Rublev painted his icons, he bore in mind that they would be viewed from far below. This explains the absence of details and the clear and concise silhouettes of the figures. The large, stooping figure of St Paul, almost completely covered by the folds of his clothes, is softly stepping and filled with inner light. The composition's colour scheme – green-blue clothes on a changing background of yellow and gold – lend it a calm and ceremonial ring.

Several icons by Dionisus and his workshop belong to the Russian Museum. *Doubting Thomas* (circa 1500) is a subject that appears

Archbishop John of Novgorod
Picture taken from his Shrine. 1559

12

in the festival tier of iconostases. This icon comes from the St Paul of Obnorsk Monastery and depicts the moment when Thomas, one of the disciples, demands physical proof of Christ's resurrection and reaches out to examine His wounds. Thomas's doubts vanish and he looks at Christ with veneration, fear and rapture. The disciple's hand and his entire stooping figure continue the line of Christ's hand, which points to His wound. Christ rises up above everyone, forgiving the unbeliever with mercy and understanding.

The Mother of God Hodigitria (1502–1503) originated in the Cathedral of the Nativity of the Blessed Virgin in the Ferapontov Monastery. It came from the local tier of the iconostasis. The clear and delicate painting of the faces, the shimmering soft-blue clothes and the golden assists and ornamental designs create the effect of inner illumination. The clear outline of the figures and their sedate gestures and poistures lend the subject majesty and purport. The meaningful centre of the icon is constituted by Christ's hand, which lies on the blue triangle of Mary's gold-edged tunic. For all its apparent rigidity and canonicity, the icon in Rus passed through various forms and stylistic devices. An important role was played by the frames adorning many icons. They often enclosed the representations in such a way that the icon took on another, richer and more decorative appearance. These settings are works of art in their own right and are now rightfully regarded as independent monuments of culture, both with their icons and separate from them. The appearance of settings was a sign of the penetration of secular principles into ecclesiastical culture. Aspirations towards dimension, ornamentation and resemblance to reality became more and more apparent in the sixteenth and the seventeenth centuries. The influence of Western originals (the Piscator Bible) was reflected in works of various schools, the Yaroslavl school in particular. A predilection for three-dimensional painting and the departure from the traditional red and yellow colour scheme were features of the works of Simon Ushakov, an icon-painter of this transitional period. Ushakov worked at the Muscovy Armoury, first as a master of silver and then as an icon-painter. He was a truly universal artist, creating miniatures for holy books, making engravings, writing treatises on icon-painting and painting both portraits (*parsuni*) and icons. The works of Simon Ushakov are noted for their depiction of dimension, following the example of the West European masters in his attempt to introduce a direct perspective into the representation. (*Y. P.*)

Simon Ushakov
The Mother of God of Tenderness of Vladimir. 1662

13

15

The Mother of God of Tenderness of Belozersk
First Half of the 13th Century

The Archangel Gabriel
(The Angel with Golden Hair). 12th Century

Boris and Gleb

Mid–14th Century. Muscovy

The Resurrection – The Descent into Hell
Late 14th Century. Pskov

The Intercession of the Holy Virgin

Mid–16th Century. Novgorod

**The Miracle of the Icon of the Holy Sign. (The Battle between
Novgorod and Suzdal).** Early 16th Century. Novgorod

19

Dionisus and his Workshop

The Mother of God Hodigitria. 1502–1503

The Almighty Saviour, shoulder-length

16th century

24

65

Dionisus and his Workshop
Doubting Thomas. Circa 1500

Andrei Rublev. St Paul the Apostle. From the
Deēsus Tier of the Church of the Dormition of the
Mother of God in Vladimir. Circa 1408. Muscovy

St George and the Dragon

Early 16th Century

St George and the Dragon. 15th Century

Greek Masters. Altar Cross
St Alexander of Svir Monastery. 1576

"In Thee Rejoiceth". Icon

Second Half of the 16th Century

The Entombment
Pall. Muscovy. Late 17th Century

St Alexander of Svir
Pall. Muscovy. Detail. 1582

32

**The Mother of God of Tenderness of Vladimir with Feast Days
and Saints.** Attributed to Procopius Chirin. Triptych.
Stroganov School. Early 17th Century

The 18th Century

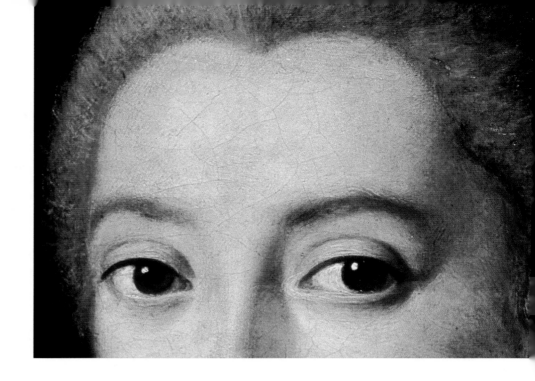

Several unique works of the transitional (from one-dimensional icon-painting on wood to three-dimensional representations on canvas) style are held in the collection of the Russian Museum. Their artistic tokens were most probably borrowed from Russia's Polish and Ukrainian neighbours. Such portraits are given the Russian name *parsuna*, meaning the representation of a concrete "person", as opposed to the saints of yore. The charm of the *parsuna* lies in its naïve union of the archaic devices of icon-painting and the attempts of the anonymous masters to conform to the European portrait genre.

Portrait of Jakob Turgenev was painted at the end of the seventeenth century. This is one of the earliest examples of *parsuna* painting. The portrait is rough and ready in its depiction of the subject's face and hands. Yet the artist was already concentrating on capturing the texture and folds of the clothes and the facial features of a concrete individual.

The end of the seventeenth century and the start of the eighteenth brought major changes to Russian life and culture. Peter the Great turned Russia towards the West and replaced the old religious ideology with a new system of Western values. Where churches and cathedrals had been built in the past, palaces and mansions now sprung up with increasing vigour.

Peter invited architects, sculptors and painters to Russia from Germany, Holland, France, Italy and other European countries. They built palaces and mansions, alongside their Russian counterparts, filling them with portraits, views and still-lifes. The early eighteenth century thus witnessed the inevitable influence of European art on Russian culture.

Peter, however, also assisted the development of Russian artists, architects and sculptors. Before the Academy of Arts was opened in St Petersburg in 1764, Russian masters received their professional schooling in various institutions, such as the Armoury and the Academy of Sciences. Several of them were accorded the honour of studying in Europe.

One such artist sent to study in Italy at the time of Peter the Great was Ivan Nikitin (circa 1680 – after 1741). Prior to this he had served at the court, painting both Peter and his wife Catherine from life.

In 1716 he and his brother travelled to Florence, where he studied at the Academy of Arts. In the early 1720s he returned to Russia at the express wish of the Tsar. He lived in St Petersburg, before moving to Moscow in 1730. In 1732 a notebook containing a lampoon on Feofan Prokopovich, Archbishop of Novgorod, was discovered in Nikitin's possession and he was arrested. He was interned as a revolutionary in the Peter and Paul Fortress until 1737, when he was exiled to Tobolsk. In the spring of 1742 Nikitin was pardoned by the Empress Elizabeth and he left Tobolsk. The exact date and place of the artist's death are unknown. Nikitin's biography paints a graphic picture of the vicissitudes experienced by artists close to the Imperial family. When power changed hands, so too did their fortunes. To be a court artist at that time was a great honour, but it could also be a personal hazard. Ivan Nikitin's fate is confirmation of that.

Nikitin's artistic heritage is small, with very few authentically signed works surviving to this day. One of his best works is *Portrait of a Field Hetman*. The history of this painting is unknown. The name of the subject has likewise never been fully established and its title is based on an inscription on the back of the canvas. There is no consensus of opinion regarding its correct translation, though it is generally taken to refer to a rank or title. Possible candidates for the figure portrayed in Nikitin's picture are various Ukrainian hetmen and Jan Kazimir Sapega, Polish nobleman who served Russia until his death in 1730. Whoever it was that Nikitin depicted in the portrait, the image created is both memorable and expressive. It is slightly reminiscent of the portraits of Titian and Rembrandt, which Nikitin saw in Italy. The dark background, illuminated face and richly painted clothes betray the hand of not just a diligent student, but also a talented master.

Alexei Antropov
Portrait of the Lady-in-Waiting
Countess Maria Rumyantseva. 1764

The europeanization of Russian culture, actively encouraged by Peter and his successors, was not the rapid and simple process that it might at first seem. The icon had dominated for almost seven centuries and had left a deep trace in Russian art. In the 1700s, as before and after, new churches continued to be built and old ones renovated. Yet this period also witnessed a break in art consciousness, with new artistic principles laid on traditional ones. It is not surprising that the careers of many masters of this time often underwent dramatic changes. One such artist was Ivan Vishnyakov (1699–1761), creator of the enchanting and enigmatic portraits of Sarah and Wilhelm Fairmore. Vishnyakov worked long and successfully as an icon-painter in the 1740s and 1750s. He also decorated palace interiors and painted plafonds, though none of these creations have survived. His portrait of Sarah Eleonora Fairmore (1740 – after 1805) is testimony to his undoubted talent and high professionalism. At first glance this picture appears to be an official portrait typical of its time. Yet the finery and luxury of the young lady's brocade and velvet apparel and her refined, somewhat theatrical poisture and gesture are combined with a touching childishness, depicted with fleeting and tender feeling. There is an undoubted proximity here to European portraits. At the same time, the works are slightly maladroit, betraying a primitive purity and inexperience of the newly assimilated devices of oil painting. The traditions of icon-painting, with its one-dimensional treatment of space and economic use of colour, are also apparent in the portrait of Sarah Fairmore. Such works naturally combine European principles with medieval features, offering a naïve picture of a wellbred young lady. Somewhat later, as in Europe, the portrait became the most popular genre in Russian art. Small chamber portraits and large official representations of the aristocracy of the day and age comprise an interesting and important part of the collection of the Russian Museum.

Despite the European orientation and obvious technical merits of the canvases of such masters as Alexei Antropov (1716–1795) and Ivan Argunov (1727–1802), echoes of medieval traditions still linger on in their portraits. These were possibly only overcome by the opening in St Petersburg of a Russian Academy of Arts in the 1760s. As is the custom in academies the world over, the young Petersburg school paid close attention to drawing, particularly from ancient and classical models. This tradition continued for a long time in the Russian Academy of Arts.

Fedot Shubin
Portrait of Paul I. 1800

The Russian Museum possesses an extensive collection of Academy drawings, tracing both the history of drawing and the history of the Academy itself. By the middle of the eighteenth century history painting had been officially established as the leading genre in art, in keeping with the hierarchy of genres common to all academies. Following the example set by European academies, where Russian masters also perfected their art, history canvases in Russia were based primarily on themes from the Bible, mythology and – rarer – pure history. The Russian Museum has a sparkling collection of Academic art, stretching from its early days right up to the 1980s. The reason for such a complete collection is perhaps its proximity to the Academy of Arts, as well as the natural prestige the Russian Museum enjoyed as the Imperial museum, always attractive to artists and collectors alike.

The museum is both curator and exhibitor of the paintings of the first Russian artists. These are the Academy professors Anton Losenko (1737–1773) and Pyotr Sokolov (1753–1791). Losenko's *Vladimir and Rogneda* played a special role in the establishment of the Russian history genre. It is based on an episode from Russian history in the tenth century. Prince Vladimir, the christener of Rus and conqueror of Novgorod, wished to take Rogneda, daughter of the Prince of Polotsk, as his wife. And despite her resistance, cunning and power, he had his way. The artist relates a love story similar to those of the mythological and biblical heroes. By introducing commoners – Russians and Poles – into the picture, Losenko lends it liveliness, national colorlit and historical authenticity. Besides history painters, the Academy of Arts produced landscape painters, masters of genre painting, portraitists, engravers, architects and sculptors. The new capital, St Petersburg, required decoration and fixation. Several albums appeared in the 1740s and 1750s, the authors of which set down the city's palaces and embankments in engravings. These engravings were later utilized by painters when transferring St Petersburg onto oil on canvas. Decorating both the outsides of buildings and their interiors became one of the most important tasks of the late eighteenth and early nineteenth centuries. Sculptors worked in various genres and materials, all well represented in the collection of the Russian Museum. Now they are unique sources of history, both of the town and its art culture.

The portrait genre was particularly popular in Russia at the end of the eighteenth century. The 1770s and 1780s represent the heyday of Fyodor Rokotov (1730s–1808), one of the most delicate and refined of portrait painters of this time. The Russian Museum possesses more than forty works by Rokotov. His *Portrait of Yelizaveta Santi (1763–?)*, painted in 1785, is one of his best. As with most of his portraits, the representation is enclosed within an oval. The texture and form of the face and the clear gauze trimming of Santi's dress are depicted by light glazing. The smoky-grey, pink and soft blue tones, Rokotov's favourites, went in perfect harmony with Rococo and early Classical interiors.

The sculptural portraits of Fedot Shubin (1740–1805), a contemporary of Rokotov, are of quite a different order. Coming from the northern region of Archangel, Shubin displayed a love of folk art his whole creative career. This is particularly evident in his carvings on bone, for which the Archangel masters were famed. His many sculptural portraits in marble also reveal his skill for working with solid materials and achieving maximum likeness to life. Shubin's portraits are not just exact physionomically. They are also personalities. The sculptor's hand transforms white marble into diverse textures and materials. Shubin was not afraid to delve into details, though these do not distract from the main thing in his portraits – the characteristics of his subject. Rather, the details help the sculptural image come to life, through a play of dimension and chiaroscuro. The Russian Museum possesses the world's most comprehensive collection of works by Shubin. *Catherine II the Legislatress* (1789), an enormous marble figure, reveals Shubin as a master of allegory and ornamentation. The statue was ordered by Prince Grigory

Dmitry Levitsky
Portrait of Glafira Alymova. 1776

Potemkin for the Tauride Palace, where it was placed in a specially built rotunda and surrounded by greenery. The ageing Empress is depicted redoubtable yet feminine, via the use of allegorical attributes and soft, lyrical characteristics. *Portrait of Paul I* (1754–1801) is an outstanding work of Russian sculpture, the artist utilizing every possibility offered by this medium. The Emperor's head is turned sharply in relation to the torso, creating an unexpected effect. Paul was a dramatic and complex figure and this is how he is depicted by Shubin – strong-willed and capricious, emotional and tearful, ugly and deformed.

Dmitry Levitsky (1735–1822) was perhaps Russia's finest portraitist of the period of Enlightened Classicism. The very ideology of the Enlightenment found sparkling reflection in his art, as illustrated in his series of seven portraits of pupils of the Smolny Boarding School for Noble Girls, painted at the request of Catherine the Great.

The Smolny Institute was opened in St Petersburg in 1764 as a privileged finishing school. It prepared the daughters of the nobility for upper-class society and service as ladies-in-waiting. The girls were educated in "socially pleasing" subjects – French, German, singing, dancing, playing on musical instruments and social etiquette. They also took part in amateur dramatics, staging per-

Grigory Ugryumov
The Election of Mikhail Romanov
as Tsar on March 14th 1613. Before 1801

formances at the Smolny Institute.

Levitsky depicted each of the girls in the roles most becoming and typical of her. Yekaterina Nelidova (1758–1839), the future favourite of the Emperor Paul, was noted for her merry disposition, grace and musical talent. In her portrait Levitsky depicts her dancing a light minuet. The grey and pink tones add lightness and charm to the image of this young individual. Yekaterina Khruschova (1761– 1811) and Yekaterina Khovanskaya (1762– 1813) are performing a scene from a pastorale. Khruschova, the elder of the two, plays the shepherd, with Khovanskaya as his young female friend. The wonderfully depicted texture of Khovanskaya's silk dress, the combination of its white-pink with the grey moire of Khruschova's caftan and the oval composition lend the scene harmony, calm and spirituality.

Levitsky painted *Portrait of Alexander Lanskoi (1758–1784)* in 1782. Like *Portrait of Catherine II the Legislatress* (1783), it is an example of an official portrait with symbolism and allegories. Alexander Lanskoi was a favourite of Catherine the Great. Raised from the ranks of the impoverished nobility to adjutant general, he was an intelligent man far removed from the world of politics. Lanskoi is portrayed alongside a bust of his patroness. In *Portrait of Catherine II the Legislatress*, the Empress is depicted in the temple of the goddess of Justice. Catherine stands beside a sculptural image of the goddess, dressed as the Legislatress. She burns poppy flowers at the altar, implying sacrifice of her personal quiet in the interests of the national welfare. Instead of a crown, she wears a laurel wreath in her hair. The decorations of the Order of St Vladimir and the books lying at her feet imply the truth and her services to her country. The sea in the distance and Mercury on the fluttering flag symbolize trade protected by the law. When *Portrait of Catherine II in the Temple of the Goddess of Justice* was finished, it won high praise from contemporaries, among them the poets Ivan Bogdanovich and Gavril Derzhavin. The portrait was ordered from Levitsky by Prince Alexander Bezborodko for his house on Pochtamtskaya Street. It later became the basis for further copies and engravings.

Towards the end of the eighteenth century the ideology of the Enlightenment began to lay increasing stress on man's proximity to nature. Large official portraits, with the subject surrounded by objects symbolizing his or her private life and public work, were however still painted. A good example is the portrait of the vice-chancellor Prince Alexander Kurakin (1752–1818), painted in 1799 by Vladimir Borovikovsky (1757–1825). The columns and draperies, the sculptural portrait of the Emperor Paul and the subject's right hand lying firmly on the official government papers speak of the position held by Alexander

Vladimir Borovikovsky. *Portrait of Vice-Chancellor Prince Alexander Kurakin. 1799*

Kurakin in the state and society. But such portraits were becoming less and less common. The vast majority of portraits painted by Vladimir Borovikovsky – more than thirty of which are now in the collection of the Russian Museum – offer an excellent reflection of the aesthetical principles of Sentimentalism. The young Yekaterina Arsenieva (1776–?), painted by Borovikovsky in the latter half of the 1790s, is carefree, sensual and coquettish. Her white tunic-like dress and straw hat in the spirit of a shepherd's reflect the fashion of those years for all things natural. At the turn of the eighteenth and nineteenth centuries the family portrait began to enjoy increasing popularity. Quiet domestic joys and the heartfelt affections of spouses, parents and children were lauded as ideal relationships, regarded then as the greatest life force. Tender kindred feelings are revealed in the portrait Borovikovsky painted in 1803 of Countess Anna Bezborodko (1766–1824) and her daughters Lyubov (1782–1809) and Cleopatra (1787–1840). The landscape background adds to the key of affable and heartfelt ties uniting mother and daughters. Landscapes painted at the turn of the eighteenth and nineteenth centuries also reflected the spirit of man's proximity to nature. Several works by sculptors working at the turn of the eighteenth and nineteenth centuries likewise display a sensual treatment of life, such as *Venus* (1792) by Fedos Schedrin (1751–1825). (*Y. P.*)

АКОВЪ : ТУРЪГЕНЕВЪ :

Unknown Artist
Portrait of Jakob Turgenev. Before 1696

Ivan Nikitin

Portrait of a Field Hetman. 1720s

Ivan Vishnyakov
Portrait of Sarah Eleonora Fairmore. Circa 1750

Ivan Vishnyakov
Portrait of Wilhelm George Fairmore. Late 1750s

Ivan Argunov
Portrait of Princess Yekaterina Lobanova-Rostovskaya. 1754

Fyodor Rokotov
Portrait of Yelizaveta Santi. 1785

48

Anton Losenko

Vladimir and Rogneda. 1770

Anton Losenko
Zeus and Thetis. 1769

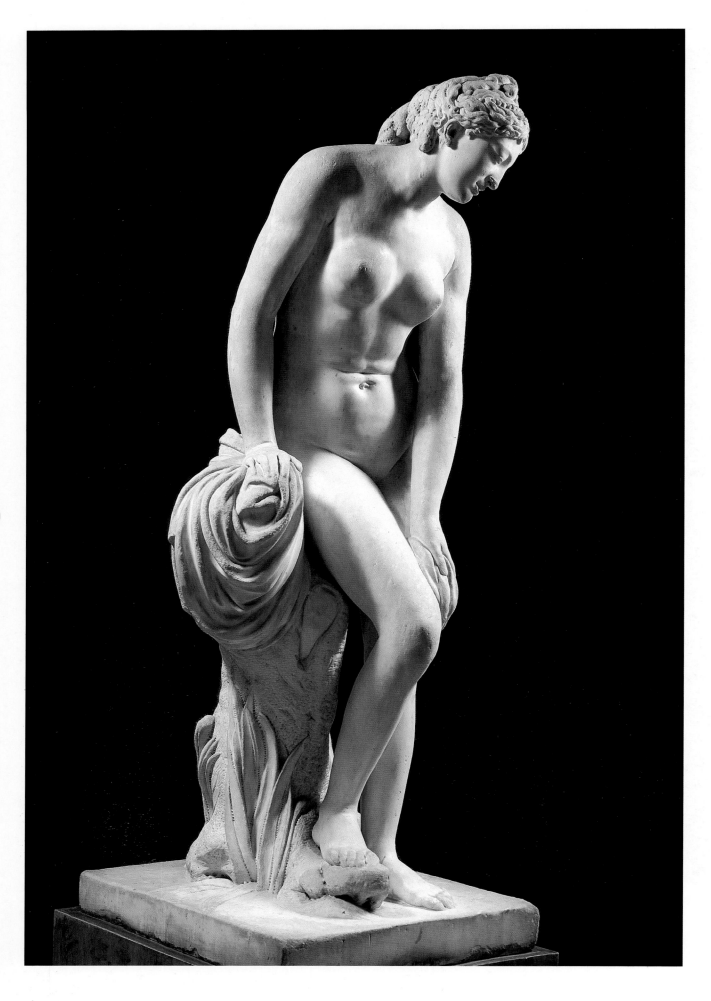

Fedos Schedrin
Venus. 1792

51

Fedot Shubin
Catherine II the Legislatress. 1789

Dmitry Levitsky. Portrait of the
Aide-de-Camp Alexander Lanskoi. 1782

Dmitry Levitsky
Catherine II the Legislatress in the
Temple of the Goddess of Justice. 1783

Dmitry Levitsky
Portrait of Yekaterina Khruschova and Yekaterina Khovanskaya. 1773

Dmitry Levitsky
Portrait of Yekaterina Nelidova. 1773

Vladimir Borovikovsky
Portrait of Countess Anna Bezborodko with
her Daughters Lyubov and Cleopatra. 1803

Vladimir Borovikovsky
Portrait of Yekaterina Arsenieva.
Late 1790s

The First Half of the 19th Century

The first half of the nineteenth century was a momentous period in Russian history. The main event was the war with the Napoleonic army, which lasted from the mid-1800s until 1814, when Russian soldiers entered Paris. The whole of Russian society was drawn into the war. General calamities and afflictions, common hopes and joys erased the social borders between classes. Aristocratic generals and serf soldiers alike proved to be mortal. The enemy burnt down peasant shacks and splendid estates with equal rigour.

Whilst the war ended with the victory of the Russian army, it left a deep trace on the outlook of an entire generation. The art of the first two decades of the nineteenth century, either directly or indirectly, expressed the new mood of society.

As an historical era, the start of the nineteenth century in Russia corresponded to the age of Romanticism in the West. As in Europe, Romanticism in Russia was never a single or united trend. Romantic works were created by both inherently Romantic artists and by masters adhering to other inclinations. Works in the spirit of Classical, Romantic, Realist and other traditions were displayed side by side at exhibitions of the Academy of Arts and, after 1824, at the Society for the Protection of Artists.

The collection of the Russian Museum offers a unique opportuntity to show the whole range of movements, trends and creative searches that existed in the first half of the nineteenth century.

In 1809 Orest Kiprensky (1782–1836) painted *Portrait of Yevgraf Davydov*, which became a specific symbol for early Russian Romanticism. The subject's aloof and dreamy air and natural yet theatrical image reflect the philosophy and manner of conduct fashionable in Russian society at the time of the Napoleonic campaign.

Kiprensky drew several works of somewhat mixed genres in the late 1800s and early

1810s. These are neither landscapes nor representations of genre scenes. His *Landscape with Barge Haulers* and other drawings are full of tense expectation of a certain alleviation after an event.

Between 1812 and 1815 Kiprensky made many sketches of soldiers who had fought in the war against Napoleon. These drawings were generally made in Italian pencil in the space of a few hours. The soldiers are portrayed in their uniforms, wearing decorations, though the focal point of these portraits are the faces, their eyes and their emotions. For Kiprensky and his contemporaries the most important object of exploration and embodiment was man's inner world. On his return from Italy and France, Kiprensky painted *Portrait of Yekaterina Avdulina* (between 1822 and 1823). This portrait, one of the finest works of Russian art in the first half of the

Orest Kiprensky
Portrait of Mikhail Lanskoi. 1813

nineteenth century, has often been compared to the works of Ingres. Both artists indeed shared a love for bold outlines. However, the Russian master's treatment of the character and emotional state of his subject in this and other portraits is less harsh, more lyrical and less distinct.

The Romantic perception of the world, which penetrated the art of the early nineteenth century, had an enormous role to play in Russian landscape painting and drawing. Previously unnoted corners of simple nature, unexpected foreshortenings and the everyday surroundings of famous monuments of

art often became sources of inspiration for Russian artists, like Maxim Vorobyov (1787–1855) – *The Neva Embankment at the Academy of Arts* (1835).

Silvestr Schedrin (1791–1830) worked in Italy alongside the painters of the Pozilippo school, creating inspired and poetic views of Rome, Naples, Sorrento and other Italian towns. The representations of the outskirts of Rome painted by Mikhail Lebedev, filled with sunshine and air, are also tinted with moods of sorrow, joy and languor.

Mention ought also to be made here of the drawings and watercolours of Maxim Vorobyov, Pyotr Sokolov and Alexander and Karl Brullov. They are kept in the museum archives yet constitute one of the bright pages in the history of Russian art. Dated the end of the 1810s and the start of the 1820s, they are full of spontaneous observations, love of nature and its poeticization in art. Romanticism, born in Russia at the start of the nineteenth century, thus underwent a number of changes, enjoying a relatively long life and combining with other trends and movements. Lyrical, intimate images of man, typical of the portraits of the early Romantic artists, united in the 1820s and in the 1830s with a garish, often theatrical, treatment of the subject. Official portraits came back into fashion in the 1820s. And the king of this genre in the Russian art of the first half of the nineteenth century was without a doubt Karl Brullov (1799–1852).

Karl Brullov's creative heritage contains a considerable number of striking portraits. One of his masterpieces is his unfinished picture of Yulia Samoilova retiring from a ball. It is more than just an official portrait; it is a pictorial symbol, a personification of the masquerade of life, where reality is often hidden from the outside eye. Karl Brullov, whilst famed as a portraitist and author of murals for several large cathedrals and churches, is best known in Russia as a history painter.

In 1823 Brullov travelled to Italy and set about seeking a theme for a history canvas. The subject of *The Last Day of Pompeii* – the most important work not only in Brullov's creativity, but also in the whole history of Russian painting – was suggested to him

Vasily Sternberg
At Grigory Tarnovsky's Kachanovka Estate. 1838

by his elder brother Alexander, an architect who had made sketches of excavations in Pompeii. Brullov spent more than five years working on his masterpiece, making numerous sketches and several painted studies. The finished picture was shown in Rome, Milan and Paris to great success. It was then brought to St Petersburg and exhibited in triumph at the Academy of Arts.

The Last Day of Pompeii has belonged to the Russian Museum ever since it first opened and is one of a rare number of completed Russian Romantic projects on an historical subject. Brullov gave bright pictorial form to the theme of tragedy so beloved of the Romantic artists. The main thematic line of the

work is the reactions and emotions of the inhabitants of Pompeii at the fateful moment. Resolving it in a major emotional and colourist key, Brullov lends the tragedy a sublime ring.

Like *The Last Day of Pompeii*, Alexander Ivanov's *Christ's Appearance to the People* was a work epoch-making in Russian art. Ivanov worked on it in Italy for more than thirty years – practically his entire creative lifetime. At its heart lies the Romantic idea of awakening, realization and perception. Ivanov chose a symbolic situation from the history of mankind – the coming of Jesus Christ and the transformation of the myth into reality – to which different people might have reacted in different ways. The artist sought long and hard for these various reactions to the appearance of Christ, painting a multitude of studies of figures, landscapes and compositional studies in the process of work on his canvas. The Russian Museum possesses a large final study of *Christ's Appearance to the People*, preceding the picture now hanging in the Tretyakov Gallery.

Important changes occurred in Russian art life in the 1820s and 1830s. The conservatism of the St Petersburg Academy of Arts had long impeded many of the vital requirements of society. Pupils of the Academy spent up to ten and fifteen years within its walls, from their very earliest childhood, and so knew little of the real world. Whilst possessing a brilliant schooling, they generally could not overcome their classical education and so their representations of real life were like theatrical scenes. Another of the Academy's shortcomings was the limitations it set on the admittance of pupils. Serfs, for example, were deprived of an art education in those years.

The answer was Russia's first private school of art, founded by Alexei Venetsianov (1780–1847). Venetsianov himself never studied art systematically. Parallel to his job as a civil servant, he studied painting under Borovikovsky and attended classes at the Academy of Arts as an external student.

In 1811 he was accorded the title of academician for a programme assignment for the Academy of Arts and was thus accepted into mainstream art life.

In 1821 Venetsianov first saw the picture of the French artist François-Marius Granet *Choir of the Capuchin Church in Rome* in the Hermitage. Stunned by the "natural" colours and aerial environment of this work, Venetsianov resolved to attain an analogical effect in his own canvases. He left for the countryside, where he painted nature and peasants directly from life. One of the first pictures shown by him at an exhibition in St Petersburg was *The Threshing Barn.*

Venetsianov achieved an effect similar to that of the French artist from the light and air filling the barn interior. In order to achieve this, he sawed away a section of the

Kapiton Zelentsov
An Artist's Room. Before 1831

barn wall and, sitting on the outside, painted the scene directly from life.

This work was of paramount significance for Russian art. For the first time in a Russian painting, peasants were depicted in their natural environment. *The Threshing Barn* opened the eyes of artists and the public to the possibilities offered by Venetsianov's method. Venetsianov's choice of nature and peasant life did not necessarily imply naturalism in his art. For him peasants and peasant life possessed their own type and ideal of beauty, confirmation of which became the essence of his art. Seeking harmony between a portrait likeness and typology, the artist drew not only from life, but also from ancient and Renaissance sources. His slightly idealized representations of peasant types, clearly not portraits, are often transformed (*Reaper, Reapers*, both 1820s) into images not unlike icons or the works of the Renaissance masters.

Regarding peasant life as the natural unity of man and nature, Venetsianov created a cycle of metaphorical pictures. Not all of them have survived down to our day. One of them is *Sleeping Shepherd* (between 1823 and 1826), personifying spring and the awakening of nature.

The confrontation between Venetsianov and the Academy of Arts was of an unaggressive nature. The artist left St Petersburg for the countryside, where he taught budding young artists, including serfs. From time to time he returned to the city to show works by himself and his pupils at Academy exhibitions.

The lives and fates of Venetsianov's pupils took different turns. After working with Venetsianov, some continued to study at the Academy and even went to Italy to perfect their art. But the brightest trace in Russian art was left by those of Venetsianov's followers who developed the theme of the Russian way of life. The representation of winter by Nikifor Krylov (1802–1831) – *A Winter Landscape* (1827) – with its simple scene of Russian peasants conversing and carrying water on yokes, is rare and inconceivable for the Academy of Arts of the 1820s.

Just as unique are the pictures of Grigory Soroka (1823–1864). The quiet

Alexander Ivanov. A Naked Boy. 1840–1850s

life of the Russian provinces with its squires and peasants are the themes depicted in the canvases of this talented serf artist. Yet the main thing in them is more than just their subjects and motifs, landscapes and interiors. Melancholy states of sadness and *joie de vivre* constitute the emotional fabrics of Soroka's works.

Venetsianov was more than just the creator of a school and teacher of many artists. His influence on the changes in Russian art was truly enormous. Exhibitions of works by Venetsianov and his students in St Petersburg led to a new fashion for depicting urban life. Artists began to increasingly paint interiors – those of their own studios, townhouses, the Hermitage and the Academy of

Arts. Echoes of Biedermeier and its extolling of private life could be seen in this craze of Russian artists. Yet there was also a natural requirement for the creation of themes, motifs and genres which the Academy of Arts had up until then disregarded. The interest of literature and music in the world of the common man and the middle and lower classes began to increasingly penetrate the fine arts. Many portraits of this time, such as Vasily Tropinin's *Girl with a Candle* and *Portrait of Pavel Vasilyev, Book-Keeper at the Bureau for the Moscow Theatres and Music-Lover* (1830s), depict those same members of the urban middle classes of the 1820s– 1840s. They echo the Russian romances and portray people from that same environment in which this musical genre was so popular. The Russian art of the 1820s–1840s was thus far from homogeneous. At the exhibitions of those years enormous canvases of a Romantic or Academic nature were often exhibited side by side with chamber works depicting scenes from everyday life. The collection of the Russian Museum offers a wide representation of virtually the entire cross-section of the art life of that time. The bright Romantic line is to be especially clearly seen in the art of such masters as Vasily Rayev (1808–1871) — *The Alexander Column during a Storm* (1834) — Karl Rabus (1800–1857) — *The Spassky Gates in Moscow* (1854) — and Ivan Aivazovsky (1817–1900). Aivazovsky painted a multitude of pictures of the sea – the fruit of his fantasy and imagination, based on personal observations. The collection of the Russian Museum contains some forty canvases by Aivazovsky, from various periods of his life. *The Ninth Wave* (1850) is one of Aivazovsky's best pictures and incarnates the Romantic concepts of tragedy, drama and eternal hope in man's victory over the elements.

The enormous number of palaces and mansions built in Russia in the eighteenth and early nineteenth centuries had to be filled and decorated. It is therefore not surprising that the first half of the nineteenth century was the golden age of Russian glass, porcelain and furniture. Besides the Imperial Porcelain Factory, founded in the eighteenth century, there were also many private factories providing all sections of the population with such

Alexander Ivanov
Three Naked Boys. 1840–1850s

necessary output. Works of applied art are one of the strongest features of the Russian Museum, setting it apart from such museums as the Tretyakov Gallery, which do not collect this type of art. These works give a representation not only of the sparkling mastery of the artists and their creations, but also the high technical standard of their produce. They paint a picture of the lives of the various classes of the epoch and their changing styles, outlooks and aesthetic and ethical values. As with literature, changes came to the fine arts at the end of the 1840s. Dramatic and sometimes even tragic notes began to increasingly burst through the soft lyrical calm of the social genre. Like Gogol and Dostoyevsky in literature, Pavel Fedotov (1815–1852) opened up the life of the *tiers état* – the military, civil servants and townsfolk – and claimed it for art. The situations depicted by Fedotov cease to be simply an object of description or narration. Almost every "anecdote" has a social subtext. One of his central canvases, *The Major Makes a Proposal* (circa 1851), versions of which are in the Russian Museum and the Tretyakov Gallery, "narrates" with light irony the popular story of the ruined aristocratic officer who attempts to improve his financial position by marrying a merchant's daughter. She in turn is rewarded with a climb up the social ladder. In several versions of *A Young Widow* (1851(2?)), Fedotov depicts a drama typical of those years, when soldiers' wives were often deprived of a roof over their heads and means of subsistence on the death of their spouses. The art of Fedotov and other genre artists of the 1840s and 1850s forms a specific bridge between the first and second halves of the nineteenth century. Themes of everyday life increasingly became the object of representation in the paintings and sculptures of these years. As before, however, the Academy of Arts continued to orientate artists on mythological, biblical and allegorical subjects, regulating the degree of lifelikeness. (*Y. P.*)

Orest Kiprensky

Portrait of Yevgraf Davydov. 1809

Orest Kiprensky

Portrait of Yekaterina Avdulina.

Between 1822 and 1823

Vulcan and Thetis.
Vase from the Ministerial Service. 1827

Pyotr Sokolov
Portrait of Yelizaveta Razumovskaya. 1817

Karl Brullov

The Dream of a Grandmother and her Granddaughter. 1829

Alexander Brullov

Portrait of Vasily Perovsky. 1824

Mikhail Lebedev
Ariccia near Rome. 1836

Silvestr Schedrin

Terrace on the Sea-shore.

Capuccini near Sorrento. 1827

Silvestr Schedrin

Naples on a Moonlit Night. 1829

Vasily Rayev
The Alexander Column during a Storm. 1834

Karl Brullov
Portrait of Countess Yulia Samoilova
Retiring from a Ball with her Adopted
Daughter Amazilia Paccini. Before 1843

Karl Brullov
Portrait of Princess Yelizaveta Saltykova. 1841

Karl Brullov
Portrait of the Poet and Playwright
Count Alexei Tolstoy in his Youth. 1836

Karl Brullov

Portrait of the Shishmareva Sisters. 1839

Maxim Vorobyov. The Neva Embankment at the Academy of Arts
(View of the Landing-stage with Egyptian Sphinxes). 1835

Boris Orlovsky
Faun and Bacchante. 1837

Alexander Warnek
Portrait of an Unknown Woman with a Red Shawl. Mid-1810s

Alexei Venetsianov

Reapers. Late 1820s

Alexei Venetsianov
The Threshing Barn. 1821(2?)

Alexei Venetsianov

Reaper. 1820s

Alexei Venetsianov
Sleeping Shepherd. Between 1823 and 1826

Nikifor Krylov
A Winter Landscape. 1827

Grigory Soroka
Fishermen. Late 1840s

Vasily Tropinin
Portrait of Pavel Vasilyev. 1830s

Grigory Lapchenko
Susanna Caught Unawares by Elders. 1831

Vasily Tropinin
Girl with a Candle. 1840s

Karl Rabus

The Spassky Gates in Moscow. 1854

Ivan Aivazovsky
View of Odessa on a Moonlit Night. 1846

Ivan Aivazovsky
The Ninth Wave. 1850

Pavel Fedotov
The Major Makes a Proposal
(Inspecting a Prospective Bride in a Merchant's Household). Circa 1851

Pavel Fedotov
A Young Widow. 1851(2?)

Vase.
Batenin Factory. Early 1830s

Vase.
Designed by Alexander Brullov.
Imperial Glass Factory. 1836–1839

The Pink Service

Flask with stopper in the form of a chapel.
Gardner Factory. 1840s.

Gilt Vase with Flowers.
Batenin Factory. 1830s

Service with Dragons.
Kornilov Brothers Factory. 1840s

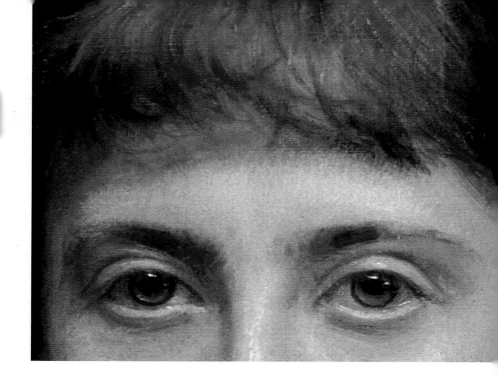

The Second Half of the 19th Century

The disparities between the realities of life and the attempts of the Academy of Arts to idealize it simmered for a number of decades before bursting into the open revolt of a group of students in 1861. They refused to paint examination pictures on mythological themes and demonstratively left the Academy, forming the Artel – Russia's first ever anti-Academic commercial art association. Its programme envisaged the reflection of real life in art and it quickly won authority. The Artel's influence was further increased by a new form of contact with the public – the organization of travelling exhibitions around Russia. The Society of Travelling Art Exhibitions was thus created in 1870 and it existed in Russia for more than four decades. "*Peredvizhniki*" was the name given in Russia to the Realist artists who joined the Society. Their works were firmly in keeping with the democratic mood of society in those years and the wave of criticism swamping every aspect of life. Amongst critical artists of those years were Vasily Perov (*The Monastic Refectory* 1865–1876, *Lone Guitarist* 1865) and Leonid Solomatkin (*Watchmen Singing Praises* 1867). The questions *What Is To Be Done?*, put by Nikolai Chernyshevsky in his novel of the same name, and *Who Is To Blame?*, muted earlier by Alexander Herzen, were hotly discussed in intellectual circles. Russian artists were also members of these circles and these issues found their way into many of the socio-critical pictures now on display in the Russian Museum.

Nikolai Ghe (1831–1894) reinterpreted the Last Supper in the light of the problems of the 1860s. His picture caused a sensation when it was revealed at the 1863 exhibition of the St Petersburg Academy of Arts. Visitors recognised Alexander Herzen, publisher of the émigré almanac *The Bell*, in the figure of the apostle Paul. The motif of *The Last Supper* had been invoked by various artists before, only now it took on a whole new and topical significance for contemporaries. They associated it with the schism that had developed in the revolutionary movement. Others interpreted the gospel subject as the tragedy of a man who foresees his betrayal by a fellow comrade, yet prepares to sacrifice himself. Ghe's picture thus transforms the biblical legend into a psychological and moral drama.

It became customary for the *peredvizhniki* to interpret the history genre in terms of modern reality. *Zaporozhian Cossacks* by Ilya Repin (1844–1930) and *Yermak's Conquest of Siberia* by Vasily Surikov (1848–1916) are more like the works of directors, reinterpreting events of old.

The majority of *peredvizhniki* were drawn to psychologism in the history genre. They read situations through experiences, reactions and the states of mind of their subjects. It is thus perhaps not surprising that the artists of the second half of the nineteenth century who painted historical themes were also fine portraitists. The portraits of Vasily Perov, Nikolai Ghe, Ivan Kramskoi, Nikolai Yaroshenko (1846–1898) and other *peredvizhniki* artists are all well represented in the collection of the Russian Museum. The range of genres

Leonid Solomatkin
Watchmen Singing Praises. 1867

and themes in the creativity of the *peredvizhniki* was extremely wide and diverse. The 1860s and 1870s were the years of the activities of the *Narodnaya Volya* (People's Will) group, a middle-class organization that sought to fight on behalf of the Russian people. Their attempts to "go to the people", meetings and acts of terrorism ended in prison, exile and death for many revolutionaries. Not surprisingly, the image of the revolutionary was popular in the democratic art of those years – *A Convicted Man* (1879) by Vladimir Makovsky (1846–1920).

The artists of those years continued to pay much attention to scenes from the life of the common people, with their everyday troub-

les and joys – Nikolai Yaroshenko's *On Swings* (1888) and Vasily Surikov's *The Taking of a Snow-Town* (1891).

Ilya Repin was possibly the most famous of the *peredvizhniki* artists, remaining so to this day. All the stages in his career in art are well represented in the Russian Museum. Repin painted *Barge Haulers on the Volga* between 1870 and 1873. It came to be regarded as a pictorial emblem of its day and age. Repin simply yet effectively resolved a theme that occupied many in those years – serf labour – uniting almost ten portraits in one composition. He does not confine himself to the portrait genre alone, though at the same time *Barge Haulers on the Volga* cannot be called a genre picture. It goes much deeper than a purely group portrait or genre scene. *Barge Haulers on the Volga* is a metaphor for strength and debility, love of freedom and the attempt to break free from slavery. The picture won the praise of the public and critics alike when it was shown at exhibitions in the 1870s. Repin was rewarded with a trip to France to perfect his art. Whilst in France, he painted *Sadko* (1876), a picture in the fairytale spirit for which he was accorded the title of academician.

Of particular importance amongst works of the 1880s belonging to the Russian Museum are Repin's portraits of the composers Alexander Glazunov (1887) and Anton Rubinstein (1887).

Many artists were friends with writers, composers and public figures, which gave birth

115

to many portraits painted in various years, such as Repin's famous representation of Lev Tolstoy (1901). The writer is depicted barefoot. It is a good portrait likeness, yet at the same time Tolstoy is likened to a lone traveller. The picture is of unusual format (207 x 73 cm), colour and composition. Its rather gloomy green-brown tones and figure standing at full height, face turned away from the viewer, lend the image an aloof and dramatic air, reflecting the inner state of Tolstoy's soul at that time.

The Russian Museum owns Repin's largest picture, *Sitting of the State Council on May 7th 1901, the Centennial Jubilee of its Foundation*, which he painted with a group of students in 1903. It was specially ordered from Repin and hung in

Ilya Repin
Job and his Friends. 1869

one of the halls of the Mariinsky Palace in St Petersburg. This group portrait is composed of more than eighty figures and demanded enormous preparatory work from Repin. He made studies of the majority of members of the State Council, also part of the museum's collection. Repin was a talented psychologist who did more than just record the outer appearances of the state elite of his time. He created a whole gallery of highly interesting characteristics of those called upon to decide the fate of Russia.

Repin was an artist forever seeking new subjects, themes, images and means of expression. He was never indifferent to events taking place in the country. Pictures such as *October 17th 1905* or *What an Expanse!* are

witness to Repin's perception, attention and interest to the new social and political moods sweeping pre-revolutionary Russia.

One of the features of the works of the artists of the late nineteenth century was attention to national manifestations in history, life and nature. Artists of those years, like Alexei Savrasov (1830–1897), closely studied local landscapes, revealing previously unnoticed poetry. The art of Ivan Shishkin (1832–1898) extols the Russian forest. After graduating from Moscow School of Painting, Sculpture and Architecture, Shishkin studied at the Academy of Arts. He went abroad in 1862 and lived and worked in Düsseldorf. Returning home, he wrote in his diary: "My motto? To be Russian. Long live Russia!" Shishkin studied nature at great length, aspiring to create an exact lifelike image. Many of his pictures encompass every single detail of nature (*A Pine Grove* 1898), though this by no means implies primitive naturalism. Amongst Shishkin's studies are no small number of genuine masterpieces of the poetic representation of nature (*Goutweed. Pargolovo* 1884(5?)). Such pictures as *Oaks* (1887) and *Winter* (1890) are lyrical and monumental images of the different states of the Russian landscape.

The landscape genre in the painting of the latter half of the nineteenth century was similar to the descriptions of nature in the Russian literature of those years. However, artists and writers did not confine themselves to visible reality. They used the state of nature to convey frames of mind and the emotional atmosphere of the surrounding world. Even such pictures as *Muscovite Courtyard* by Vasily Polenov (1844–1927) – the pictorial tale of a little corner of Moscow – are tinged with fresh perception of an everyday subject. Polenov was not a landscape painter. Like many at this time, he painted pictures on historical and biblical themes (*Christ and the Adultress* 1888), as well as genre and landscape works. This syncretism reflected the logical development of the art of the second half of the nineteenth century, with biblical and historical motifs coming to life in a plausible environment. The landscape was on the whole a relatively diverse and rich phenomenon

Ilya Repin
The Raising of Jairus's Daughter. 1871

in Russia in the latter half of the nineteenth century. It ceased to be simply a view, inspired by the artist's emotional and philosophical perception of nature. It often crossed beyond the borders of its genre, transformed into a pictorial metaphor for Russia, as in *Thaw* (1871) by Fyodor Vasilyev (1850–1873). Romantic traditions (Ivan Aivazovsky, Alexei Savrasov, Fyodor Vasilyev) were quite strong in the landscape genre. Unusual even for this type of artistic outlook were the works of Arkhip Kuindzhi (1842–1910). Kuindzhi was of Greek origin and introduced that measure of artistic relativity and laconic brevity found in the art of the turn of the century into his landscapes of the 1870s and 1880s. He was not so much interested in landscapes, views or objects as in

light and colour at various times of the day and night, in summer and in winter.

Isaac Levitan (1860–1900) also occupies a special place amongst landscape painters working in the second half of the nineteenth century. His works are often compared to the prose of Anton Chekhov, a personal friend of the artist and a writer who had a similar outlook on life. Levitan searched for the "soul of Russian nature" in his art. His works are devoid of views. Instead, the artist's creative face is defined by the "mood landscape", expressing a whole range of emotions, from pessimism to notes of optimism. Meditations on life and man through nature and the elements are typical of Levitan's best works now in the collection of the Russian Museum (*Golden Autumn. Suburb* and *Twilight. The Moon* 1899). The late nineteenth and early twentieth centuries was a stormy period in the history of Russian art, with the appearance and development of various trends. As before, artists turned to social themes – *The Poor Gathering Coal in a Worked-out Mine* (1894) by Nikolai Kasatkin (1859–1930) – continuing the themes that had occupied the *peredvizhniki*.

Other artists, like Vasily Vereschagin (1842–1904), followed their own personal paths in art, ones without precedent in Russian painting. Vereschagin was widely travelled and a witness of many battle scenes. The subjects of his pictures are war and its tragedies and the lives of the peoples of various nations (*At the Doors of a Mosque* 1873). (*Y. P.*)

Vasily Perov
The Monastic Refectory. 1865–1876

Ivan Kramskoi

Portrait of Sofia Kramskaya, the Artist's Daughter. 1882

Ivan Kramskoi

Mina Moiseyev. 1882

Vasily Maximov
Dreaming of the Future. 1868

Vladimir Makovsky

A Convicted Man. 1879

Vasily Surikov
Yermak's Conquest of Siberia. 1895

Vasily Surikov
The Taking of a Snow-Town. 1891

Ilya Repin
Preparing for an Exam. 1864

Nikolai Yaroshenko

On Swings. 1888

Henryk Semiradsky

Phryne at the Festival of Poseidon in Eleusin. 1889

Ilya Repin

Barge Haulers on the Volga. 1870–1873

Ilya Repin
Portrait of the Composer
Anton Rubinstein. 1887

Ilya Repin
Portrait of the Composer
Alexander Glazunov. 1887

Ilya Repin

Sadko. 1876

Ilya Repin

What an Expanse! 1903

Ilya Repin
Lev Tolstoy Barefoot. 1901

Ilya Repin
Zaporozhian Cossacks. 1880–1891

Ilya Repin
Centennial Sitting
of the State Council. 1903

Vasily Polenov
Muscovite Courtyard. 1902

Vasily Polenov
Overgrown Pond. 1880

Vasily Polenov
Christ and the Adultress
(Who is Without Sin?). 1888

Ivan Shishkin
Winter. 1890

Ivan Shishkin
A Pine Grove. 1898

Ivan Shishkin
Gout-weed. Pargolovo. 1884(5?)

Ivan Shishkin

Oaks. 1887

Fyodor Vasilyev
Thaw. 1871

Arkhip Kuindzhi
Patch of Moonlight in a Forest.
Late 1890s – Early 1900s

Arkhip Kuindzhi

Evening in the Ukraine. 1878

Isaac Levitan

An Overcast Day. 1895

Isaac Levitan

Twilight. The Moon. 1899

Nikolai Kasatkin
The Poor Gathering Coal
in a Worked-out Mine. 1894

Abram Arkhipov
Laundresses. 1901

Vasily Vereschagin
Shipka-Sheinovo
(Skobelev outside Shipka). Before 1890

The Turn of the Century

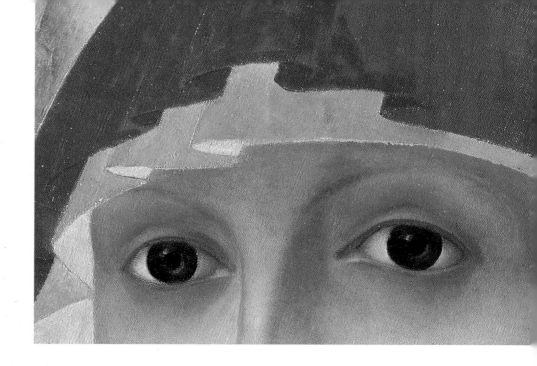

An interesting aspect of Russian art at the turn of the century was its revival of interest in Russian history. Not only historical subjects, but fairy-tales, legends and artists' fantasies on themes from national history also became the subjects of pictures. *A Knight at the Crossroads* (1882) by Victor Vasnetsov (1848–1926) belongs to Russian epos. *A 17th Century Moscow Street on a Holiday* (1895) and *A Merchant's Family in the 17th Century* (1896) by Andrei Ryabushkin (1861–1904) are compositions on themes drawn from life in the Russia of the seventeenth and eighteenth centuries. Ryabushkin's humorous treatment of the Russian way of life stands in light contrast to the pathos commonly encountered in history works.

This renewed interest in Russian life later told on the art of other masters. Boris Kustodiev (1878–1927) portrayed the lavish life-style of the provincial merchant class (*A Merchant's Wife* 1915, *Shrove-Tide* 1916, *A Merchant's Wife at Tea* 1918). Philipp Malyavin (1869–1940) created exotic images of the early twentieth century Russian

peasantry. Clothed in bright shawls and sarafans, they went down in Russian art history as the *Malyavinskiye babi* (Malyavin's peasant women).

Mikhail Vrubel (1856–1910), like Valentin Serov, Mikhail Nesterov, Boris Kustodiev and many other twentieth century masters, began his career at the end of the nineteenth century. He found inspiration in Russian fairy-tales, traditional heroic poems (*Bogatyr* 1898) and works of literature (*The Demon*). The one important difference, however, was in his interpretation of these motifs. Vrubel's artistic tongue and images went beyond that which was traditional for the nineteenth century. The hypertrophically exaggerated figure, highly decorative landscape and untraditional format differ *Bogatyr* from other works based on fairy-tale themes.

Vrubel's construction of form through brush-strokes in his mosaic *A Six-winged Seraph* (1904) broke new ground in the representation of the real and imaginary world. Vrubel destroyed all classical notions of form and composition. Vrubel was a well-educated artist who gave new meaning to many literary heroes. One of them was Lermontov's "demon", which Vrubel believed was often wrongly mistaken for the chort ("horned" in Greek) or devil ("slanderer"). Demon in Vrubel's translation means "soul". The image of the "demon" is one of the central themes in Vrubel's art. *A Sitting Demon* (1890) and *A Fallen Demon* (1902) belong to the Tretyakov Gallery. The Russian Museum possesses several illustrations to Lermontov's poem, as well as the picture *A Flying Demon* (1899).

Like many other of Vrubel's works, *A Flying Demon* is associated with the ideas of Symbolism. Incarnation of the spiritual and creation of a new language of symbols was a typical feature of the art of the turn of the century. Vrubel's demon is "mournful and melancholy ... imposing and imperious". Its outstretched figure soars above the earth, burning eyes scrutinizing the world below. The indeterminate form, intricate colours and unusual composition set this work and many other of Vrubel's canvases apart in the history of Russian art. Valentin Serov (1865–1911) was a close friend of Mikhail Vrubel. Both studied in Pavel Chistyakov's studio at Moscow School of Painting, Sculpture and Architecture. Although principally a portraitist, Serov did not confine himself to this genre. He also painted poetic landscapes (*In Winter* 1898) and history compositions (*Peter II and the Tsarevna Elizabeth Riding to Hounds* 1900).

Valentin Serov
Peter II and the Tsarevna
Elizabeth Riding to Hounds. 1900

Serov both followed and developed the classical line in Western and Russian painting, adding typically Impressionist searches in colour and light. The most brilliant aspect of Serov's art is his portraits, which come in various sizes, colour schemes and compositions. Serov was merciless when painting his models. Lavish settings and expensive clothes could not mask his feelings towards the subject. Zinaida Yussupova (1902), Felix Yussupov (1903) and Olga Orlova (1911) all appear cold and haughty in their official portraits painted by Serov. Olga Orlova was so displeased with her portrait – a true masterpiece by the artist – that she lost no time getting rid of it, presenting it in 1912 to the Alexander III Museum (now the Russian Museum). In 1907 Serov travelled to Greece with Léon Bakst (1866–1924). This journey brought a decisive influence to bear on Serov's art, for after it he turned to archaic art, reliefs and the murals of Greece and Egypt. Towards the end of his short life, Serov created several works in a completely new style, such as *Portrait of Ida Rubinstein* (1910).

Ida Rubinstein was a dancer with Diaghilev's *Ballets Russes*. Serov depicts her naked, with a complete lack of idealization. If anything, he exposes and accentuates the sharp, angular forms of her body. The picture is like a poster or a mural, terse in colour and drawing. Serov spurns details and surrounding environment, concentrating all his attention on the eurhythmics that capture the true spirit of Ida Rubinstein. Konstantin Korovin (1861–1939) was a follower of the Impressionist line in art and a close associate and contemporary of Serov and Vrubel. He painted landscapes and still-lifes, as well as theatrical designs, decorative panels and portraits. Korovin preferred to paint the portraits of people with whom he was already well acquainted. One such model was Tatyana Lyubatovich (1880s), an opera singer who sung in performances staged at Savva Mamontov's private opera house.

Korovin, Vrubel, Serov and other artists were often guests at Mamontov's estate in the village of Abramtsevo. By the end of the nineteenth century it had become a major centre of the arts and haunt of writers, painters and artistes. It was here that Korovin first met Lyubatovich. Her portrait is more than just the representation of an individual. Under Korovin's brush, Lyubatovich becomes an image for femininity, youth and inspiration. Fyodor Chaliapin, the famous singer, was also a friend of Korovin's. Korovin painted his portrait in 1911, depicting a lively and contented individual.

An association which took its name from the periodical it published – *Mir Iskusstva* (The World of Art) – played an important role in Russian culture at the turn of the century. The history and way of life of Holy Russia and Old Europe were themes developed by Alexander Benois (1870–1960), Yevgeny Lanceray (1875–1946), Konstantin Somov (1869–1939) and Mstislav Dobuzhinsky (1875–1957), all of whose works are well re-

Léon Bakst. *Portrait of Sergei Diaghilev with his Nanny. 1906*

presented in the collection of the Russian Museum. These artists did more than just bring gallantry and refinement together with humour and the grotesque in Russian art. They also extended the borders of the active participation of leading masters in the art process. The design of book covers and stage sets (particularly for Diaghilev's *Ballets Russes*) became one of the most important activities of the members of the *World of Art* group.

Theatrical passions clearly reflected on the stylistics of easel art in the works of masters who helped design stage sets, artists like Léon Bakst and Alexander Golovin (1863–1930).

Golovin depicted Chaliapin in the role of Boris Godunov in Mussorgsky's opera of the same name. As in his other works, elements of theatricalization and the stylistics of curtains and costumery predominate. Bakst's *Terror Antiquus* (1908) is also reminiscent of an enormous curtain. The same can be said of his portraits (*Supper* 1902, *Portrait of Sergei Diaghilev with his Nanny* 1906), which whilst not entirely traditional, are nevertheless still painted in the spirit of easel compositions.

Following on from *The World of Art*, other groups of artists began to appear in Russia, each of them with its own programme and direction. Victor Borisov-Musatov (1870–1905) headed an association going by the poetic name of *The Blue Rose*. His light-toned and lyrical works feature a departure from reality into the world of reverie and day-dreams.

The works of Pavel Kuznetsov (1878–1960) – still-lifes, portraits in landscapes and romantic Oriental scenes – are close in colour scheme to those of Borisov-Musatov. Oriental themes were prominent in the works of many artists working at the start of the twentieth century. The brightest of them was Nikolai Roerich (1874–1947), a pupil of Repin and then Kuindzhi. He had a deep interest in history, philosophy and travel, sailing around the Great Water-Way as a young man (1899).

Pictures of the Russia of the past had then sprung up in his imagination.

Drawing on impressions gained from his travels, Roerich painted a cycle of pictures dedicated to Rus's Varangian period (*Overseas Guests,* 1902).

In 1923 Roerich went on an expedition to Central Asia, after which he founded a scientific research institute in India to study the Himalayas. A whole series of Roerich's works are devoted to these mountains and he spent the last years of his life in India. When in Russia, he presented the Russian Museum with his enormous heritage of some two hundred works.

Neoclassicism — or Neoromanticism, as it is sometimes called — was another of the highly original phenomena of early twentieth century Russian art. At a time when innovative explorations in form were very much in vogue, artists like Alexander Yakovlev (1887–1938), Vasily Shukhayev (1887–1973) and Zinaida Serebryakova

Konstantin Korovin
Portrait of the Singer Fyodor Chaliapin. 1911

(1884–1967) sought inspiration in the works of medieval and Renaissance masters. They were to a certain extent following a path similar to that of the Pre-Raphaelites. Modern subjects are lightly stylized in their works in imitation of the pictorial and plastic tongues of their great predecessors. Interest in the Russian theme is noticeable in the works of Serebryakova and Boris Grigoriev (1886–1939).

The start of the twentieth century saw the widespread influence of modern Western art on Russia. Russian artists travelled widely across Europe, while Moscow and St. Petersburg were home to the private galleries of Savva Morozov and Stepan Schukin. These contained paintings by Cézanne, Matisse and other twentieth century innovators at a time when they had still to achieve world fame. All of this rendered an undoubted influence on the path and nature of Russian art.

Followers of Cézanne soon appeared in Russia. They formed a group bearing the revolutionary name *Jack of Diamonds* and reinterpreted "Cézannism" in a highly original and typically Russian manner.

The still-lifes, portraits and landscapes of Ilya Mashkov (1881–1944), Pyotr Konchalovsky (1876–1956), Alexander Kuprin (1880–1960) and Aristarkh Lentulov (1882–1943) utilize the pictorial, plastic and thematic tackiness of Russian folklore art (shop signs, toys, pulp fiction) alongside devices typical of Cézanne. Now they are held in museum collections, including that of the Russian Museum, on an equal footing with their pictorial canvases. At the end of the nineteenth century distaffs, trays, wooden and clay toys, embroidered towels and clothes were merely part of the everyday life of peasant households. The *Jack of Diamonds* artists resurrected them as works of art in their own right. A widespread phenomenon at the start of the twentieth century was a return to Russia's national roots. The bright and vivid works of Mashkov, Lentulov and Kon-chalovsky invoked folk motifs and traditions and were displayed at exhibitions alongside the pictures of Boris Kustodiev, which poked fun at the merchant class, and the philosophical meditations on Russia of Mikhail

Victor Borisov-Musatov*. Self-Portrait with Sister (Elena Borisova-Musatova). 1898*

Nesterov (1862–1942). Nesterov's images glorified the ascetic life of hermits and the common spirituality of those who have withdrawn from modern life.

Kuzma Petrov-Vodkin (1878–1939) passed from a period of interest in French Symbolism to deep delvings in Russian themes and searches for national means of expression in the 1910s. His sources of inspiration were Russian icons, with their predominance of red, and the Russian countryside, with its blue sky and green expanses. Petrov-Vodkin's works are diverse in genre, composition and content. His severe, almost ascetic still-lifes, portraits, genre compositions and thematic representations of military events

are similar to icons and linked to the history of Russia and events taking place in it.

The great surge of works on Russia's past and present, interpreted in many unexpected, original and different ways, resulted in a multi-coloured kaleidoscope of the various styles in the art of the turn of the century. Such diversity did not, however, imply decline or confusion. On the contrary, it testified to the free, full-blooded and unfettered nature of Russian culture at the start of the new century. It is not surprising that this period witnessed the maturing and formulation of aesthetic ideas, ones principally new for the art of the twentieth century.

The Rayonism of Mikhail Larionov (1881–1964), the abstract art of Wassily Kandinsky (1866–1944) and the Suprematism of Kazimir Malevich (1878–1935) and associates all owe their appearance to the abundance of non-abstract art. The Russian Museum owns a fine collection of Russian avant-garde, representing practically every trend, name and movement in this branched process that confirmed the new aesthetical ideas and means of artistic expression.

Mikhail Larionov and Natalia Goncharova (1881–1962) were possibly the first to depart from the narrative nature of the old art and place accent on simplification of form. Attention to the folk art of various countries, among them Russia and the Ukraine, enriched the palette and plastics of these artists and left a bright trace in Russian art. Nathan Altman (1889–1970) and Marc Chagall (1887–1985) lived long creative lives, progressing from an initial interest in French Cubism. Even their early works carry the spark of their creative independence. Their works of the mid-1910s rank amongst the best examples of Russian avant-garde — Altman's *Portrait of Anna Akhmatova* (1915) and Chagall's *Promenade* (1917). Wassily Kandinsky, after an initial interest in Expressionism, officially proclaimed his adherence to abstract art in 1911. The Russian Museum possesses more than twenty works by Kandinsky, which trace his development from Expressionism to abstract art. Kandinsky orientated himself on sensations born of the subconscious. Form in his works is defined by colour, rhythm and spots. Here Kandinsky was close to the icon-painters and masters of folk art, from whom he derived much inspiration. Malevich came to his personal revelation of Suprematism via Impressionism, Cubism and Cubo-Futurism. His heritage (more than a hundred pictures and some twenty drawings) is better represented in the Russian Museum than anywhere else

Konstantin Korovin. *Portrait of the Actress Tatyana Lyubatovich. 1880s*

in the world. The pictures of his Impressionist and Symbolist periods, the Cubo-Futuristic *Portrait of Kluhn* (1911) and *Aviator* (1914), his Suprematic compositions of 1915 and 1916 and his series of peasant men and women of 1928–1932, uniting figurative art with Suprematism, are the pride of the Russian Museum. Just as complete and unique is the collection of works by Pavel Filonov (1883–1941). Almost two hundred pictures and more than two hundred of his drawings and water-colours were presented to the Russian Museum by his sister, Yevdokia Glebova. Filonov developed his own personal technique, to which he gave the name "analytical". It can be traced from his early compositions (*Shrove-Tide* 1913(4?) and *The German War* 1915), which reveal Filonov's bright individuality alongside noticeable links with folklore, right through to his mature works. Filonov arranged his pictures like plants growing in nature. His compositions were often similar to mosaics or pictures in a kaleidoscope. Yet beyond the form – original and aesthetically attractive – lay profound, philosophical meditations on man and the surrounding world. (*Y. P.*)

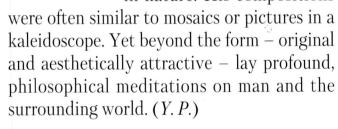

Andrei Ryabushkin

A 17th Century Moscow Street on a Holiday. 1895

Andrei Ryabushkin

A Merchant's Family in the 17th Century. 1896

Andrei Ryabushkin

A 17th Century Muscovite Girl. 1903

Victor Vasnetsov

A Knight at the Crossroads. 1882

Mikhail Vrubel

Bogatyr. 1898

Mikhail Vrubel

A Six-winged Seraph. 1904

Mikhail Nesterov
The Great Taking of the Veil. 1898

Mikhail Nesterov

Hermit. 1888

Léon Bakst

Supper. 1902

Mikhail Nesterov
Portrait of Olga Nesterova, the Artist's Daughter. 1906

Alexander Golovin

Portrait of Fyodor Chaliapin in the Role

of Boris Godunov in Mussorgsky's Opera of the Same Name. 1912

Léon Bakst

Terror Antiquus. 1908

Alexander Benois
Commedia dell' arte. 1906

185

Alexander Matveyev

A Youth. 1914

Konstantin Somov
Winter. Skating-rink. 1915

Konstantin Somov

Portrait of Elena Pits-Bilibina. 1926

Valentin Serov
Portrait of Count Felix Sumarokov-Elston,
later Prince Yussupov. 1903

Valentin Serov
Portrait of Princess
Zinaida Yussupova. 1902

191

Valentin Serov

Portrait of Princess Olga Orlova. 1911

Valentin Serov

Portrait of Ida Rubinstein. 1910

Nikolai Roerich

Overseas Guests. 1902

Nikolai Roerich

Remember!

Philipp Malyavin

Peasant Women. 1905

Ilya Mashkov

Portrait of a Boy in a Painted Shirt. 1909

197

Boris Grigoriev

Portrait of the Producer Vsyevolod Meyerhold. 1916

Zinaida Serebryakova

A Bath-house. 1913

Boris Grigoriev
Girl with a Milk-churn. 1917

Marc Chagall

Red Jew. 1915

199

Marc Chagall
Promenade. 1917

Vasily Shukhayev and Alexander Yakovlev
Self-Portraits (Harlequin and Pierrot). 1914

203

Alexander Yakovlev
Violinist. 1915

Pavel Kuznetsov
Sheep-shearing. Circa 1912

Pavel Kuznetsov
Still-life with Crystal. 1910s

Kuzma Petrov-Vodkin

Thirsting Warrior. 1915

Kuzma Petrov-Vodkin
Morning. 1917

Kuzma Petrov-Vodkin
Mother. 1915

Kuzma Petrov-Vodkin

The Mother of God of Tenderness Towards

Evil Hearts. 1914–1915

Aristarkh Lentulov
Self-Portrait in Red. 1913

Aristarkh Lentulov

Churches. New Jerusalem. 1917

Lady under a Parasol. Clay Toy. Tula. 1880s

Three Distaffs. Late 19th Century

Cellar Door from the Zhdanovs' House. 1892

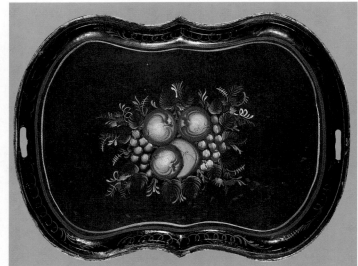

Tray. Perezolov's Workshop, Nizhny Tagil. 1887

Sledge. Vologda Province. 1915

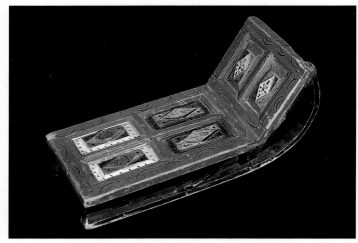

Female Costume (Blouse, Pinafore, Top).
19th – Early 20th Centuries

Distaffs. Various Russian Provinces. 19th–20th Centuries

Anton Melnikov. Nizhny Novgorod Province. Detail.
Distaff. Mid–19th Century

Sledge. Vologda Province. Early 20th Century

Alexander Guriev
Spring in the Tundra. Vase.
Arkhangelsk Region. 1977

Window Casing, Jambs and Lintel. 1890s

Natalia Goncharova
Peasant Women. Circa 1910

Natalia Goncharova

Peasants. Late 1900s

216

Mikhail Larionov
Barber. Late 1900s

Natalia Goncharova

Cyclist. 1913

Mikhail Larionov

Venus. 1912

Mikhail Larionov

Yellow Autumn. 1912

Nathan Altman
Portrait of the Poetess Anna Akhmatova. 1915

Ilya Mashkov

Portrait of a Lady with Pheasants. 1911

Nathan Altman

Portrait of a Young Jew (Self-Portrait). 1916

Beatrice Sandomirskaya

Portrait. 1920s

Boris Kustodiev

A Merchant's Wife at Tea. 1918

Boris Kustodiev
Merchant's Wife with a Mirror. 1920

The 20th Century

History is like the depth of the ocean waves. The further you delve into the depths of the past, the less movement is noticable to the eye. The closer one gets to modern times, the more perceptible is the clash of movements. Finally, there is the surface of the current day, where the waves crash and play, distorting and destabilising the picture.

Our understanding of twentieth century art history is equally distorted. And the century is by no means over. Many years must pass before everything can be classified in neat cells and a lasting system of definitions and boundaries drawn up.

The only thing that can be said with certainty is that the collection of the Russian Museum is diverse and complete enough to bring together the various fragments to form an objective and detailed picture of Russian twentieth century art. The special pride of the museum is what is possibly the world's largest collection of Russian avant-garde. The heart of this collection of some 400 priceless works was put together by the avant-garde artists themselves – Kazimir

Malevich, Mikhail Matiushin, Vladimir Tatlin and Pavel Mansurov. In 1921, in the wake of the revolutionary transformations, they attempted to create an equally revolutionary Museum of Art Culture where, as Malevich hoped, "the old concept of the artist will vanish and in its place will appear the scientific artist."

The experiment was short-lived. The Communists had by then established their authority and were ill-disposed towards the revolutionary games of the "scientific artists". The artists themselves proved to be too colourful and individualistic to work together as one team and soon fell out. In 1926 the unique collection they had put together was handed over to the Russian Museum.

The museum's collection of Russian avant-garde continued to grow, despite the growing state persecution of "Formalist" artists. The collection grew out of personal tragedy too, like in 1942, when the museum was presented with practically the entire heritage of Pavel Filonov, who had died of hunger in the siege of Leningrad. One of the important recent additions has been Malevich's *Partial Eclipse. Composition with Mona Lisa.*

It was only *glasnost* and *perestroika* that finally allowed this collection to be "declassified" and brought out into the light of day. At last the Russian Museum could offer the world a glimpse of the hidden treasures of early twentieth century art. Its numerous exhibitions, including *Art Groups of the Twenties and Thirties* (1989) and *The Great Utopia* (Germany, Holland, USA, 1992–1993), finally laid an end to the crude division of Russian art into "pre-revolutionary" and "post-revolutionary". These exhibitions showed the genetical link between avant-garde and the Russian art of the end of the nineteenth century. The latter represented a period of the completion of a definite and perhaps even biological cycle. It was a time of the toppling of authorities and the downfall of ideas and ideals, ones that had once been progressive but which had now become tired and overworked, reverting into dogma and stereotypes. Today, one can see that the situation at the turn of the century was a mirror image of the situation two hundred years earlier. Then, at the turn of the seventeenth and eighteenth centuries, the Russian artist had liberated himself from the rigid canons of icon-painting, free at last to apply the revolutionary new possibility of the "life-like" depiction of man, objects and the world. The wheel then turned full circle at the start of the twentieth century. Russian art, having destroyed or transformed figurative form beyond all

Kazimir Malevich. *Study for a Fresco Painting (Self-Portrait). 1907*

recognition, returned again to the icon (Malevich's *Black Square* and *Budetlyani*, Filonov's *Holy Family* and Goncharova's *Evangelists*). The difference was that this time it was not to religion as such, but to its emblematic system.

The tragedy of revolution and two wars (the First World War and Civil War) at the start of the twentieth century could not help but act as a powerful catalyst for the changes taking place in Russian culture. By the start of the 1930s, however, the "art born of the revolution" had become the art of Socialist Realism.

Two important events took place in the offical art life of the early 1930s.". The first was the Party resolution *On the Restructuring of Literary and Art Organizations.* This spelt an end to the activities of a whole host of art groupings, as well as to the short-lived and fragile alliance between avant-garde art and the Communist regime. The second was the opening, first in the Russian Museum and then in Moscow, of the large jubilee exhibition *15 Years of Artists of the RSFSR.*

Sergei Luchishkin, one of the artists featured in the exhibition, recalls, "The whole exposition was divided into three sections. The first and largest of the three consisted of works which, in the opinion of the organizers, answered to all the principles of Soviet art. The second section, the smallest in size, was located in the following hall. Here were the 'fellow-travellers', those who had still to decide where their allegiances lay. And finally the third section, works by artists 'infected with various Formalist diseases and the influence of the bourgeois past'." This was the ideological hierarchy established by the Party, categorizing all artists into three types – officially recognized, semi-recognized and officially unrecognized. This hierarchy similarly defined the equally simple and rigid structure of Soviet art life. There was also a parallel system of official values, defining the relative importance of themes, genres, subjects, motifs and heroes.

Exhibitions of the officially recognized artists were the main source for additions to the museum collection – though not the only one. There was in addition a shadow department, one that also grew, though not without difficulties. This "salon of lepers" was unknown to the general public, yet well-known to the artists themselves, artistic circles and the Party "curators". Its size varied in relation to the level of concern for the ideological purity of the style and method approved by the Party.

It is thanks to this department that when organizing its series of exhibitions dedicated to the art of the Stalin years half a century later, the museum was still able to provide an objective view of the society of those years. For Soviet citizens not only engaged in "double-think"; they did so intentionally, deliberately forming an unobjective and contradictory picture of their own lives. The museum collection therefore paints a true picture of the era and its art. And not only in the form of the official propagandist publications, exhibitions and placards that bombarded the Soviet public from all directions in those years. It also includes works that could be seen – albeit only by a few privileged visitors – in the studios of the disfavoured artists, those who had walked

Olga Rozanova
Street. 1910s

"the ideologically incorrect path of Formalist searchings".

At the end of the 1940s, after two decades spent in battle with "Formalism", the party ideologue Andrei Zhdanov would still lament, "It is completely intolerable. Alongside the art of Socialist Realism coexist tendencies which regard the French Formalists Picasso and Matisse, the Cubists and the artists of the Formalist *Jack of Diamonds* group as their spiritual teachers". This alone proves that far from everything in the Soviet art of those years was subject to the "all-seeing eye" of the Party. The art of the 1930s–1950s was far more than just portraits of faceless party leaders and enormous statues staring into the future. There was also the continuation of the fine traditions of Russian Realism, the tenacious development of Russian avant-garde, and a wonderful art schooling, which produced many of the masters of the 1960s–1980s.

The final years of Stalinism in Russia were the first years of a new wave of bright young stars in Russian cultural life. Shostakovich's *Ninth Symphony* was performed for the first time, Yevgeny Mravinsky was conducting in Leningrad, Prokofiev's new ballet *Cinderella* was premiered at the Bolshoi Theatre, Rudolf Nureyev was dancing on the Kirov stage, Eisenstein's *Ivan the Terrible* was shown in the nation's cinemas and Tvardovsky was publishing Solzhenitsyn in *Novy Mir*. The first post-war competition of musicians was won by the young soloist Svyatoslav Richter and the Conservatoire student Mstislav Rostropovich. Those artists who later set the course for the development of the fine arts in the 1960s–1980s either made their debuts or completed their education in those years. It was they who pursued the Minimalist style that appeared in the latter half of the 1960s, on the heels of the Khruschev "Thaw". This style too is well represented in the collection of the Russian Museum, thanks to acquisitions from the less bombastic yet just as well organized exhibitions held all over the Soviet Union in those years.

Less fair stood things in the underground movement. Too many of its artists were driven into emigration and too many of their works scattered across the globe – too many even for Russia and the twentieth century. But, as it is written in the Bible, "The wind blows to the south, it veers to the north; round and round it goes and returns full circle." In recent years the museum has launched a determined programme to return their names and works to Russia, in order to complete the picture of Russian art life in the 1970s and 1980s. These artists are now well represented in "The Ludwig Museum in the Russian Museum". This is a collection of works presented to the museum by the well-known German art collectors Peter and Irene Ludwig, designed to provide a sensation of the general context and give impetus to modern Russian art. The collecting policy of the Russian Museum reflects its traditional belief that besides maintaining and upholding classical traditions, it cannot and must not stand aloof from current affairs. All the more so when the current situation re-

Alexander Samokhvalov
The Militarized Komsomol. 1932–1933

quires the museum to play a more active social role. Pavel Florensky's idea of a "living museum" once again acquires topicality. It was he who wrote of the necessity of "taking the museum out into life and injecting life into the museum." Just as topical is the concept of Nikolai Punin, who headed the museum's Department of Modern Art in the 1920s. He wrote that museums, in light of the recent changes, "will inevitably assume the duties of shaping and regulating modern art life ... the old museum, the depository of the arts, will be forced to broaden and radically change the direction of its activities." The Russian Museum has in recent years restored the Department of Modern Art, closed down at the start of the 1930s. In doing so it has become the first museum in Russia to place modern art in the traditional museum space. The purchasing and exhibitionary policies of the museum are aimed at filling in the gaps in its collection — the heritage of the years of Communism, when political diktat distorted the true picture of the art process. Moscow and Petersburg underground, lyrical conceptualism, soc-art, conceptual photography and forms of post-modernism are now being actively collected. The Department of Modern Art is particularly geared towards radical and avant-garde works. And today the museum cannot imagine its existence without this intake of "fresh blood" and the impulse that it gives to the more traditional forms of museum work. (*V. G., Y. P.*)

Vladimir Tatlin

Artist's Model. 1910s

Vladimir Tatlin

Sailor. 1911

Wassily Kandinsky
St George. 1911

Wassily Kandinsky
Improvisation. 1910

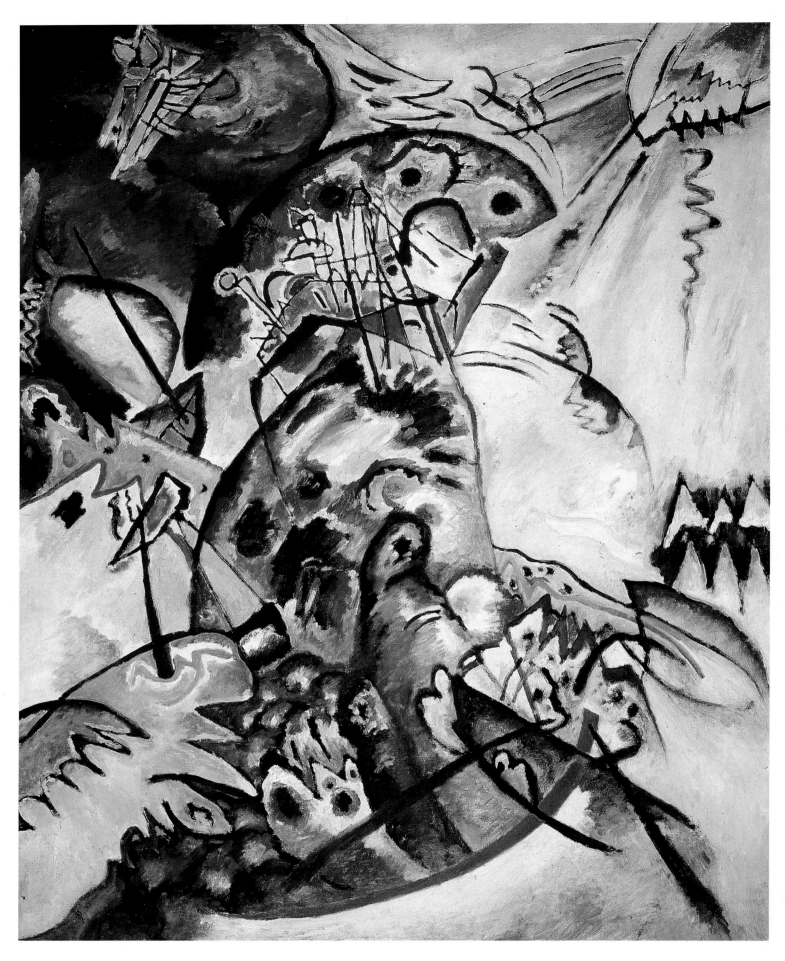

Wassily Kandinsky
Blue Crest. 1917

Wassily Kandinsky

Composition. 1920

237

Kazimir Malevich

Aviator. 1914

Kazimir Malevich

Partial Eclipse. Composition with Mona Lisa. 1914

Kazimir Malevich

Suprematism. 1915–1916

Kazimir Malevich
Suprematism. Female Figure. 1928–1932

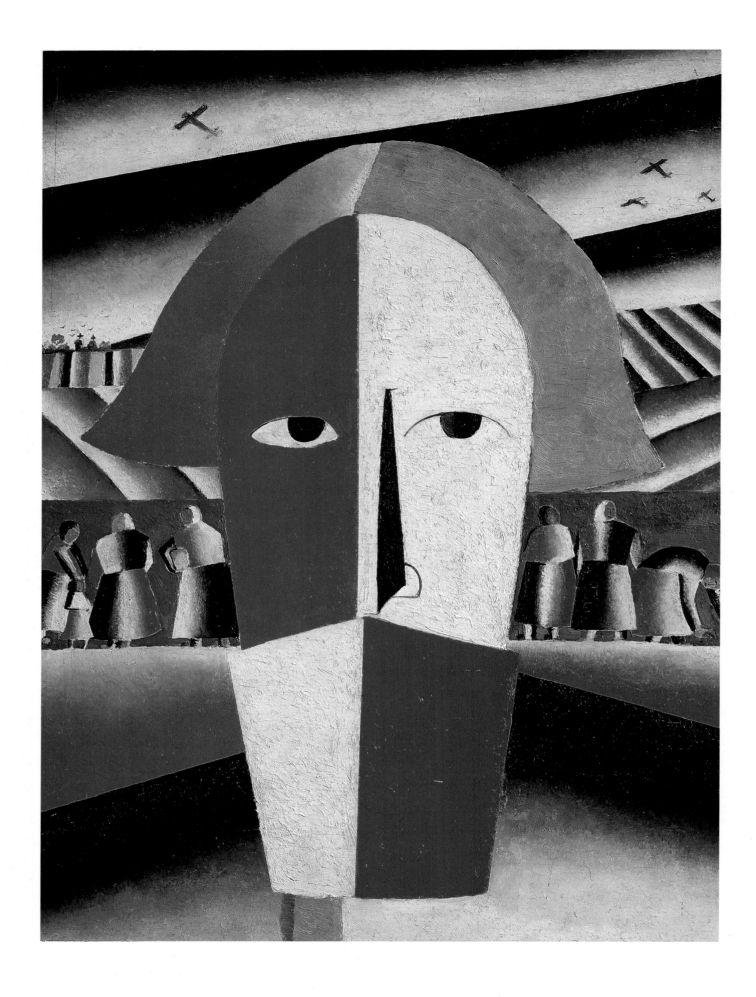

Kazimir Malevich

A Peasant's Head. 1928–1932

Kazimir Malevich

Girls in a Field. 1928–1932

Olga Rozanova
Abstract Composition. Mid–1910s

Olga Rozanova

Writing-table. 1910s

Ivan Kluhn

Ozonizer. Mid–1910s

Lyubov Popova
Man, Air, Space. 1915

Pavel Filonov
Peasant Family (The Holy Family). 1914

Pavel Filonov

Banquet of Kings. 1913

Ivan Puni
Still-life with Table. 1919

Ivan Puni

Still-life with Letters. 1919

Alexander Samokhvalov

Conductress. 1928

Alexander Deineka

Textile Workers. 1927

Alexander Deineka
The Defence of Sebastopole. 1942

Alexander Gerasimov
Hymn to October. 1942

Yury Kugach, Vasily Nechitailo, Victor Tsypalkov
Glory to Great Stalin. 1950

259

Dmitry Zhilinsky
Under an Old Apple-Tree. 1969

Victor Ivanov
Family. 1945. 1958–1964

Helium Korzhev

Conversation. 1980–1985

261

Yevsei Moiseyenko

In Memory of a Poet. 1984

Nikolai Sazhin
Moidodyr. 1982

Olga Bulgakova

Buffoons. 1979